M000315406

Before the Borderless

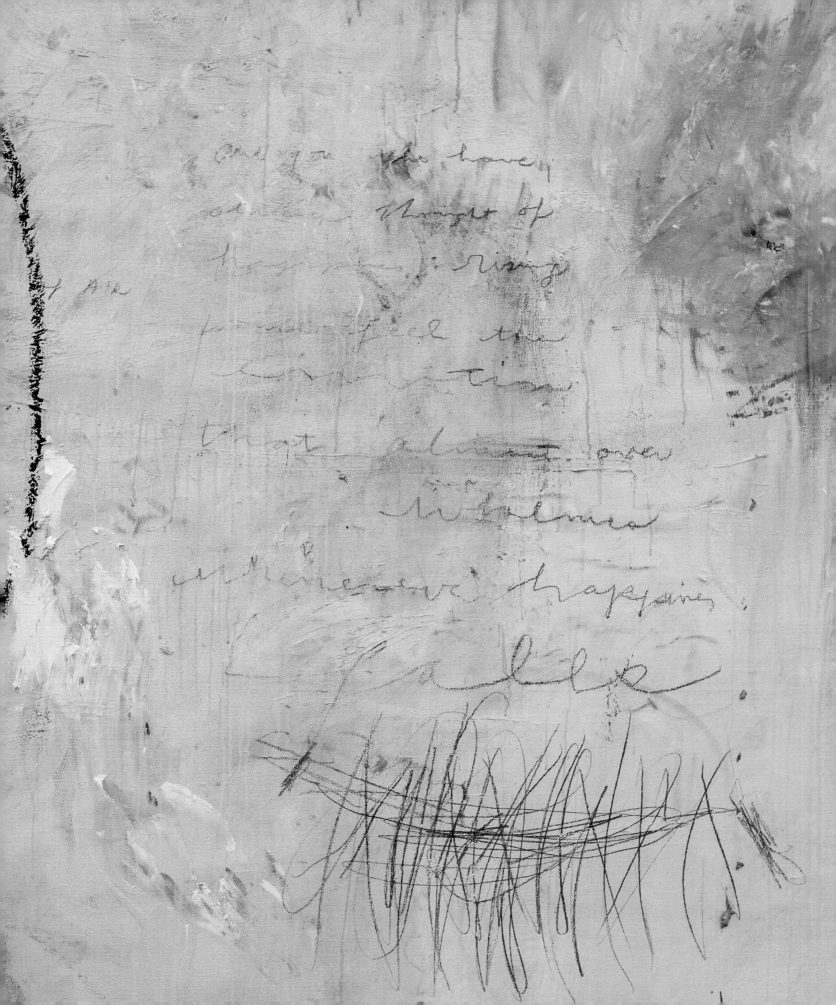

Before the Borderless: Dialogues with the Art of Cy Twombly

Dean Rader

COPPER CANYON PRESS

PORT TOWNSEND, WASHINGTON

Copyright 2023 by Dean Rader
All rights reserved
Printed in Canada

Cover art: Cy Twombly, Installation view of *Untitled (Say Goodbye, Catullus, to the Shores of Asia Minor)*, 1994. Oil, acrylic, oil stick, crayon, and graphite on three canvases, 157 ½ × 624 in. (400.1 × 1585 cm). Courtesy of the Menil Collection, Houston. Gift of the Artist. © Menil Foundation, Inc. Photograph by Paul Hester.

Frontispiece: *Untitled (Say Goodbye, Catullus, to the Shores of Asia Minor),* detail, center panel, 1994

Copper Canyon Press is in residence at Fort Worden State Park in Port Townsend, Washington, under the auspices of Centrum. Centrum is a gathering place for artists and creative thinkers from around the world, students of all ages and backgrounds, and audiences seeking extraordinary cultural enrichment.

LIBRARY OF CONGRESS CATALOGING-IN-PUBLICATION DATA
Names: Rader, Dean, author.
Title: Before the borderless : dialogues with the art of Cy Twombly / Dean
  Rader.
Description: Port Townsend, Washington : Copper Canyon Press, [2023] |
  Summary: "A collection of poetry by Dean Rader"— Provided by publisher.
Identifiers: LCCN 2022048190 (print) | LCCN 2022048191 (ebook) |
  ISBN 9781556596759 (hardcover) | ISBN 9781619322707 (epub)
Subjects: LCSH: Twombly, Cy, 1928-2011—Poetry. | LCGFT: Poetry.
Classification: LCC PS3618.A3476 B44 2023 (print) |
  LCC PS3618.A3476 (ebook) | DDC 811/.6—dc23/eng/20221206
LC record available at https://lccn.loc.gov/2022048190
LC ebook record available at https://lccn.loc.gov/202204819

9 8 7 6 5 4 3 2 FIRST PRINTING

COPPER CANYON PRESS
Post Office Box 271
Port Townsend, Washington 98368

www.coppercanyonpress.org

This book is in memory of my parents:

Gary Dean Rader (1946–2017)

Ginger Rader (1947–2022)

Contents

Before the Borderless

I

I never really separated painting and literature.

Cy Twombly

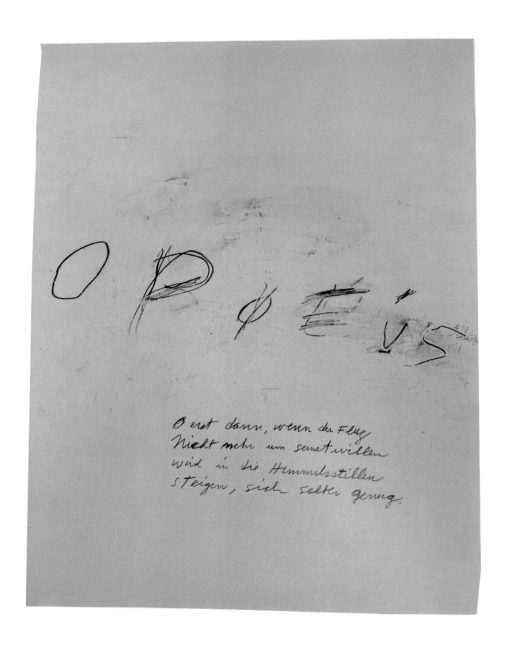

Orpheus, 1979

Troubled by Thoughts about Infinity and Oblivion, I Exit the Twombly Retrospective at Dusk
and Walk the High Line with the Ghost of My Father

This evening, the unknown waves its wand,
                              and a beam of light disappears into the sky's black hat.

The moon has never known its true home.
The stars do not remember when they began their journey.

Out of that forgetting,
                  they begin their own making.

Just like us.

Soon the sun will take off its cape
                              and open a door to a place that is not there.

Out of that absence,
                  the questions:

What black bones hang above the unseen?
What name does the fire give to flame?
What burns through existence to endlessness?

We are not here long enough to believe in anything but language,
and yet we know what awaits us is silence—
somehow always rising above the darkness
                              into darkness,
always drawn to our own obscurity.

Future self,
          I think of you arriving at our ending—
last line on the last page—
                  the trace within the vanishing,
the final sleight of hand in which everything disappears.

Remember: the unseen is never truly empty.

Despite erasure,
                  the canvas never blank.

Untitled, 1970

In Which Twombly and Rader Consider the Letter

In the beginning was the word,

      and the word was with

the letter: the letter / is the beginning &

        in the beginning

is the letter: first mark, first slash, first line, first

sign—not drawn but notched,

      scored: the spoor of speech:

the trace, the track /

      of utterance:

the invitation not just to see but to read,

      to record: to write

and rewrite the self into everything it is

      and is not: letter within letter:

line from writer to reader:

      sender / receiver:

what is life but a correspondence—a notation

written / read by & about the self:

      Dear X, Dear Y—

Life, like the sentence,

      ends, but what if the letter is infinite?

lettir, leitre, Anglo-Norman and Old French, Middle French *letre, lettre,* Anglo-Norman and Middle French *lectre* (French *lettre*) (in plural) knowledge or learning acquired by the study of written texts, erudition (10th cent. in Old French; in Anglo-Norman also in singular (beginning of the 14th cent. or earlier)), any of the symbols of an alphabet, inscription, text (ca 1160), precise words of an utterance or document, exact or literal meaning of something (ca 1170), written communication addressed to a person or group of people, epistle (ca 1170 in plural *lettres;* in Anglo-Norman, Old French, and Middle French frequently in plural; first half of the 14th cent. or earlier in singular), official or legal document (1234; in Anglo-Norman, Old

Dear Twombly—

       Master of the eternal *e,* unending *o*—

what letter would you write to /

for our country? What sign / what scrawl

speaks through its own silence into the ear

of our brightest hearing?

          Calligraphic and metonymic

all at once. Yes, it is true we may not hear,

but we still might read,
          and yes, it is true that we may

not read, but we still might see.

Darkness blinds, but only until it is marked by light.

Blindness darkens,

       but only until it is lit by mark.

What awaits us, Cy,

       in the mailboxes of the dead?

Here, the glyphs and graphemes

of our daily lives seem at best unreadable,

       at worst struck through.

It is time to draw the insurgent word /

       time to write the letter of our uprising on

the envelope that is this land.

To the tyranny of edict,

       I send the erasing angel:

To the president of autocracy,

       I post the cancellation.

French, and Middle French frequently in plural), writing, lettering (beginning of the 14th cent. or earlier), individual block of type (1486), (in plural) study of grammar, rhetoric, and poetry (1538); classical Latin *littera* (also *litera*, (in inscriptions) *leitera*) letter of the alphabet, letter as pronounced, letter as written, character, style of lettering, script, short piece of writing, (plural *litterae*) elements of education, written form or matter, text of a document, letter of the law (as opposed to the spirit), document, record, inscription, epistle, literary works, writings, literary pursuits, scholarship, erudition, in post-classical Latin also sacred literature, scripture (late 2nd cent. in Tertullian), charter, deed (from 8th cent. in British and continental sources), of unknown origin; the hypothesis that it is connected with *linĕre,* to smear, is now generally rejected.

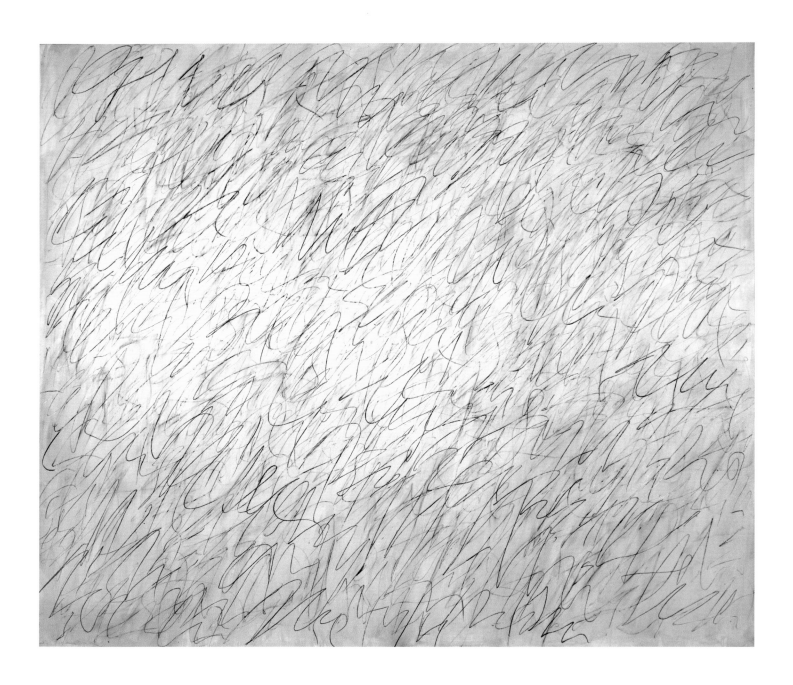

Nini's Painting, 1971

Meditation on Comprehension

Our lives are illegible,

                        why not this page?

Obsession and exploration on an endless loop—

                                                                        [what are these marks?]

I'm tired of typing the word *marks*—

                                        I want to write the word *word*—

                                                [though words are themselves marks of their own failure]

                                                        Slash, scrape, sketch—

everything always a trace toward understanding.

                                                                Query:

                        Is it possible to record what we do not see?

                Is it possible to see what we do not read?

Is it possible to read what we cannot write?

                                                                Proposition:

                                                        All seeing is a form of believing:

                                                        All belief is a mode of feeling:

                                                        All feeling is a line of thinking:

What I don't understand,
                        I still might read

What I am unable to read,
                        I still may understand.

Note I from *Three Notes from Salalah*, 2005–07

Meditation on Absolution

My heart:
green

as a lake
but not

as smooth.
White noose

after white
noose—

will I swing
or will I

sing the
words of

my note
to the

depths?
What will

I not
say? To

what will
I not kneel?

Beyond (A System for Passing), Part X, 1971

System

black line

        blank page

did I write *page*? I meant *canvas* [so I typed *page*]

[I am beginning to believe that everything might be a mark of its own making]

did I write *write*? I meant *draw* [watch me write *line*]

[*if it is not written is it beyond being read?*]

Did I write *word*? I meant *image,* so I drew *line*

What is a sentence but a line of words drawing us toward absence?

What does it mean to *write* a *line*?

[To solve the problem of language] you need language.

Untitled, 1970

Meditation on Instruction

I

In Twombly's *Untitled* you don't know where to look, because you can't figure out which way the surface is moving. At first you believe it begins at the top of the canvas, almost in mist, before spiraling down toward you. But then you see the direction is upward, a landscape in reverse, scaling a shifting mountain of stone and debris, until it disappears into the clouds. Vast swirl of stasis and motion, umber erasure of the heavens.

II

When I look at this painting, I see Oklahoma, I see autumn, I see wheatfields, I see the sun and a ray of rust and the wind bending the stalks but at the same time mending them into something akin to skin smoothing itself over a body that is not there, internal swirl of the not-yet-cut, glume and awn, spike and stem, glazed gold in the long rake of late light, all spiral, all coil, here tiller and rachis, here the ligule of last leaf.

III

How many fields go fallow inside me? Do you recognize me, wind, blind in the emptiness made by your moving?

IV

This is one of the few scribble paintings Twombly executed in earth tones. Color is its own language, its own metaphor. Imagine the same composition but in blue or green. Imagine this poem in stanzas. Imagine the dead deep below the surface of the field: the roots of the stalks stretching toward history as the little tips in the bright breeze make their own marks in infinite space.

V

In 1970, Twombly is 41 years old. He paints this in Rome where, 41 years later, he will die. This piece makes me think of death: the palette of harvest: the season receding into the long barrow of winter: the harrow hard into ground: the nights numberless, cold and countless: the orange and ash and flesh and flint and fall: the silent shift from stem to soil: that last release: the unlocking leaf: the slash of sickle and scythe: the brush lifting from the canvas: the pencil pausing:

VI

When I was a boy, my grandfather walked me around the rim of our family farm. Wheat and more wheat. Nothing but wheat. Barely soil, barely a hill. It was Sunday. He was still wearing a tie. His shirt was the color of the wheat: his tie brown as the dirt the wheat bequeathed. If you stand here long enough, he said, you will learn everything you need to know. I, who always wanted to be taught, asked him if he thought god could learn anything new. He put his hand on my shoulder, and we walked into the stalks like two figures stepping into a story from an ancient book that is yet to be written, into the blank spaces where illustrations would go. The page, like the world, is always waiting to be known. When god looks at my life, the lord learns nothing from me but infinite regret. But when the lord looks at this painting, it is god who learns about light.

Untitled, 1967

Meditation on Circulation

How does a line point to where it does not go?

How does a note rung into an empty room remind you of silence?

How is anything a sign of what it cannot be?

        Our days are a tiny book that can never be filled,

no matter how much we write

        or how little we erase.

Is there any secret in skulls, asks Stevens,

        things go round and again go round.

Nothing on this earth is straight—

        not the sky, the sea, the self—

Even colors curve

        in the light of their swerve toward the other—

What does not begin can never end,

        but in one's ending lies the trace of beginning.

I think of you,

        lineated self,

in the unending blankness beyond the beyond:

        repetition its own beauty—

Ode to Psyche, 1960

Sonnet: The Inscrutability of Influence

Mid-hush'd, cool-rooted—

these tuneless numbers of pale-mouthed prophets,

tender-eyed, aurorean . . .

one only adds new ink.

The human heart is a grid

in the midst of this wide quietness—

—this heart—

repository of all writing.

What is a poem?

Neither form nor usage––

neither urn nor autumn:

bones burn,

leaves light and lay down their matches.

A pencil lifts a hand.

Untitled, 1969

Unending Octet

unraveled yarn, scribbled egg, broken slinky
on the pavement, inverse hills, nonsense circuit, bowed
grass, curled barbed wire, graffiti teeth, tumbleweed
bone, sky writing, *o* throw, ladle spill, blood roll
saddle stitch, spaghetti curl, white whirl, ash
death spring, infinite *e,* chalk chain, unending bone-
spring, yarnstitch, *o* bend, slinky ash, unending wire
on the pavement, chalk ash, scribbled death loop, infinite lasso

Mars and the Artist, 1975

Meditation on Revision

All abstraction is a form of incompletion-—

       all incompletion an ~~exit to~~ emptiness.

    Nothing can be said ~~enough.~~

         All art a form of silence—

a~~ll~~ prayer ~~a mode of not hearing~~—

     To those who ask, god reveals ~~himself through~~ absence,

~~to those who do not~~ he stays silent.

        Still, we ~~feel the red~~ bleed ~~blue~~.

Cold Stream, 1966

Meditation on Motion

The line like the river does not know to stop

neither does my wonder

I would like these lines to be drawn on my skin

I would like to feel these lines beneath my skin

a current alternating between my body

and the earth galvanized with meaning

charged with inscriptions of infinity like us

o beloved to flow with you through this life

and after the elegant simplicity of effusion

our motion lost in the rolling waves that carry

us out encirclement and continuance and

the connection of everything drawing us in

beloved we don't have to be beautiful to be beauty

Untitled, 1966

Studies for Excursus

And it goes like this, says Tityrus:
And it goes into the into.
And it goes out on a horse.
And it goes like victory,

                says The Into:

So many have galloped,

                barebacked, into themselves.
So many have taken both the blue pill and the red pill.
So many are anvil hearted,

              hammer hearted.

So many removed their arms so their hands could not be nailed,

                      thousands.

Untitled (Variations on the Elegies), 1966

Elegies (Variations)

I

One among us in
darkness. There is no
place we can remain
alone in this life.

II

Does the infinite space
we dissolve into know
our breath, our skin-
shape, our last first?

III

Death is pacing this
poem like a panther
in a cage. Mother,
you made him small.

IV

The dying must notice
how real real grief
can be. Mother: this
whole life is elegy.

V

The language that begins
duration, that names mourning:
O show me the
place words lift light.

VI

A word is elegy
to what it signifies.
Through this falling, I
sing your continual ascent.

VII

Valéry. Rilke. Like you,
I am lone before
God. Nowhere will world
be but within us.

VIII

I remember you the
way forest recalls rain
after fire. Dearest Ghost,
free from burning, rise.

IX

Twombly's box [once for
each thing] is the
shape, Mother, of the
bed you died in.

X

The emptiness around them
the scale of the
stars—the space where
one day I find you.

Ginger Rader, In Memoriam (1947–2022)

II

All artworks are writing.

Theodor Adorno

Poems to the Sea, 1959

Meditation on Mimesis

The tree outside

        my window

  looks exactly

      like a tree.

Out the back window,

  the ocean

      resembles a photograph of a cloudy sky

  minutes after rain.

        If I close my eyes I see the ocean

          better than if they were open.

          Is it possible to never know exactly what we see?

      When the dawn-lean light leans

  against the limbs

        of the dead

    boxwood at the end

  of the street

     it is easy to imagine.

   How deep can one go

into an idea?

The color

of *nature*

is green,

even though so

much is not.

Is any symbol not aspirational?

Is anything ever really empty?

Once the great desert was a great ocean.

Can you see it?

Things, says Kant,

that we see are not by themselves

what we see.

How deep can one swim

into what one is not?

How long does the wind spend

sharpening its knives?

My alien craft has nowhere to land

and so it has set down in the

unexplained—

A fisherman will spend an entire

life looking at what he cannot see

and yet he is not blind.

The plovers gather

on the sand like a memory,

and yet the waves have not once recalled the grass.

Science, says Plato,

is nothing but perception.

What do we know

of that which is not inside?

Fifty Days at Iliam: Shield of Achilles, 1978

The Fire That Consumes All before It

No man is set above or below the condition common to all men; whatever is destroyed is regretted. Victors and vanquished are brought equally near us; under the same head, both are seen as counterparts of the poet, and the listener as well.

Simone Weil on Homer's *The Iliad*

I

Burns

    along the blue—

        burns

    on the skin—

        the sky a sea of swimming arrows:

explosions: shield and shade:

        shuddering along the edges of everything:

below: men in ships

        and the sky a spume of sparks,

everything a light:

        Listen to the tree

            flame.

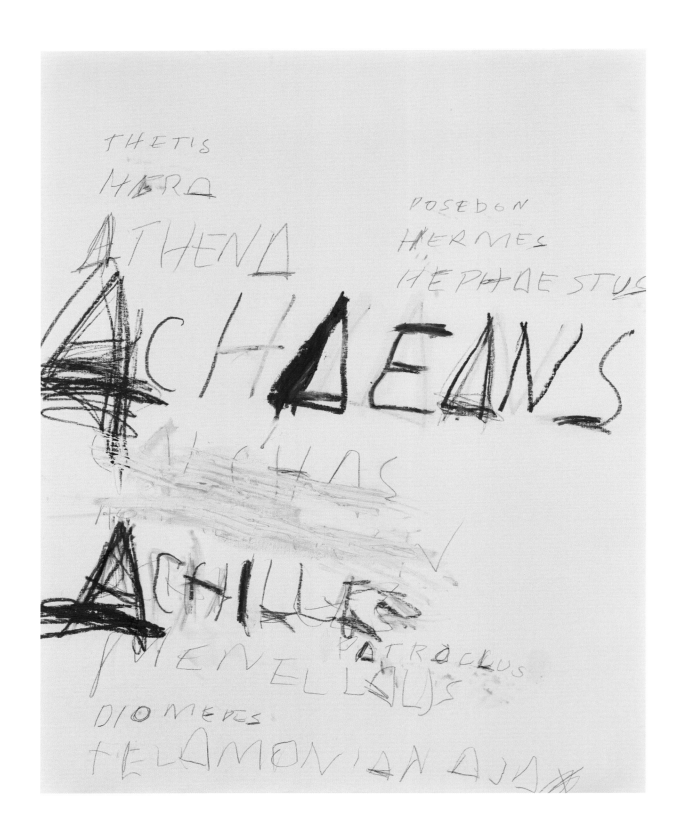

Fifty Days at Iliam: Heroes of the Achaeans, 1978

II

Listen to the tree flame

into the sound

that is this praying

mouth:

What do the gods ask of the men who ask the gods to hear them?

What prayer,

what voice goes voiceless

into the void?

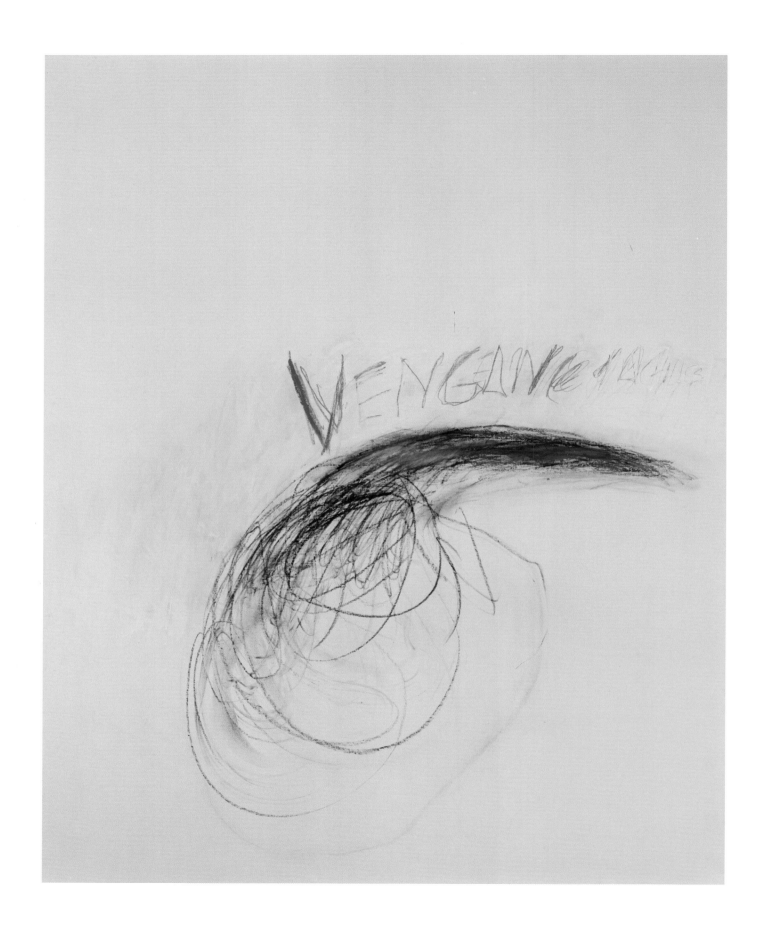

Fifty Days at Iliam: Vengeance of Achilles, 1978

III

                                                            Into the void:

        into branches of bone

                                        into blood bloom and cartilage loam:

                into soil swirl,
                                a hurl in

to night

            breaking

        back
                to the ground of its making,

                                        making the path of

    wrath and reprisal
                        the torch that lights
                                        through its scorch

        history's black trunk.

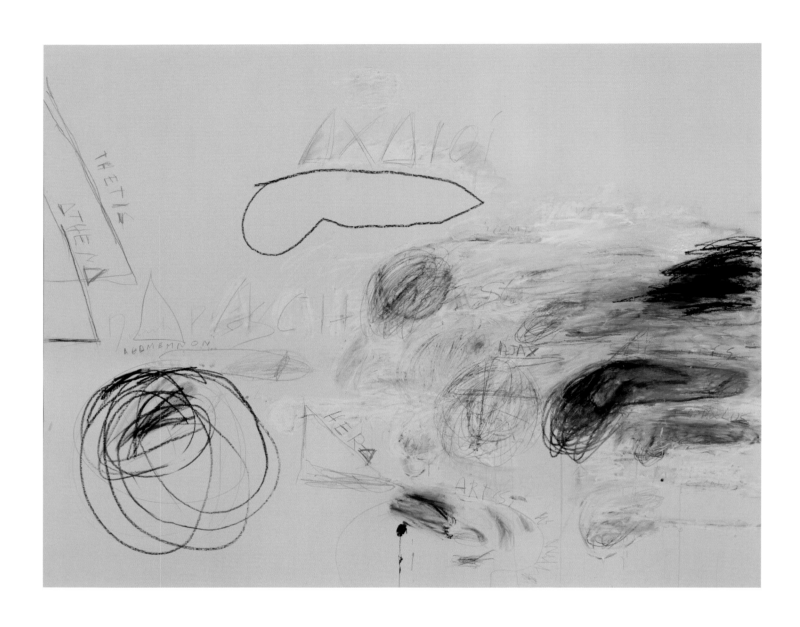

Fifty Days at Iliam: Achaeans in Battle, 1978

IV

History's black trunk:

the dead's red roots:

the spear in your hand:

the blur of blue and bow

beneath your skin.

Time is never an arrow

except in those flashes

of flight

when it is.

Fifty Days at Iliam: The Fire That Consumes All before It, 1978

V

When it is

in a poem,

the moon is a bone of pure music and

the heavens a bruise and the stars tiny torches.

Or maybe the stars are the dead—

distant flames firing deep into themselves,

the night sky

nothing more than

the blackened wings of angels.

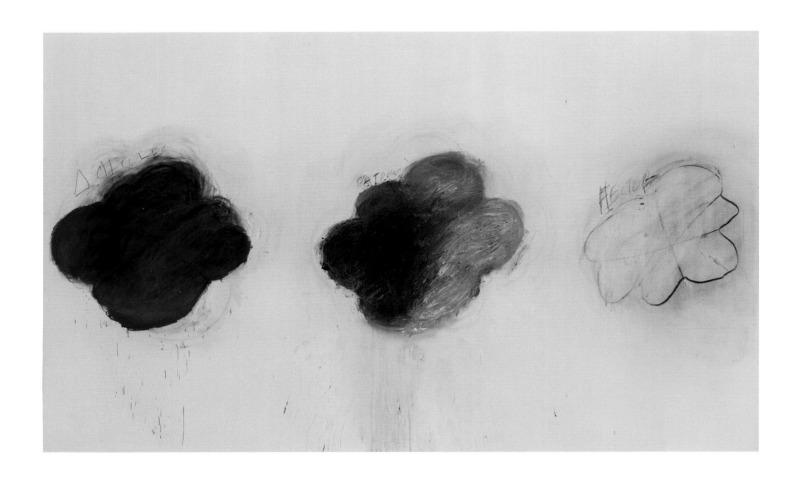

Fifty Days at Iliam: Shades of Achilles, Patroclus, and Hector, 1978

VI

The blackened wings of angels,

                    quiet as the moment before god

speaks

                           silence:

      word as the reversal of speech,

                        the inhalation of all that is not sung—

]sun   ]shadow   ]shade

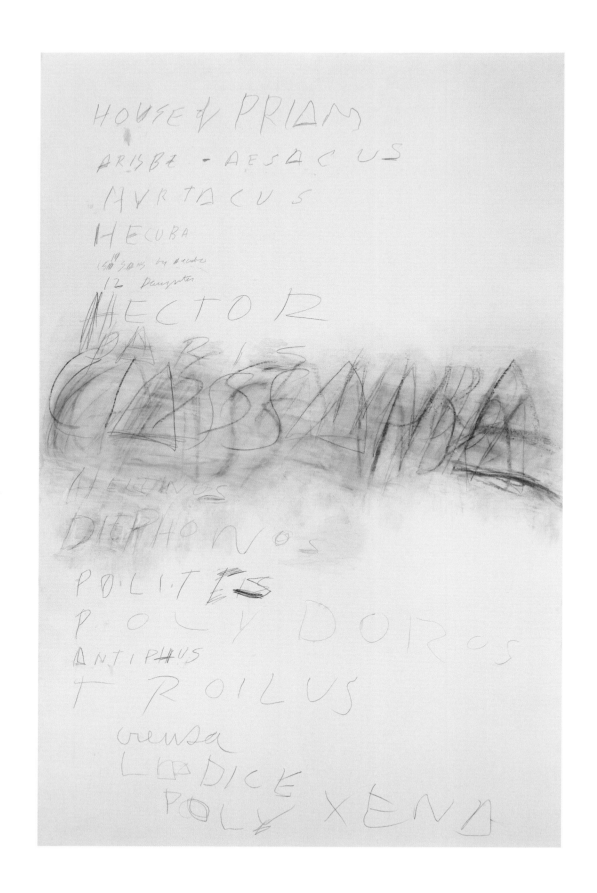

Fifty Days at Iliam: House of Priam, 1978

VII

Sun→Shadow→Shade→

the other side of sound:

[Homer→Pope→Twombly→Rader]

pages fade:

names erase:

[Samuel Johnson on Pope's *Iliad*→*the noblest version of poetry which the world has ever seen*]

For a king's pride, people perish:

[*Declare, O Muse! in what ill-fated hour*
Sprung the fierce strife]

Roll back,
                    O lord

of language,

the stone of speaking:

return once more:

Fifty Days at Iliam: Ilians in Battle, 1978

VIII

Return once more

to the ship of your own making, making

your way into the way—

shield after shield after shield:

body among body among body among body among body among body among body among body:

What will men not do?

Who will men not kill?

Bodiless names / nameless bodies:

What hasn't been written?

What has been remembered?

What hasn't been broken?

Fifty Days at Iliam: Shades of Eternal Night, 1978

IX

What hasn't been broken

may yet one day be:

Not just war but the idea of war:

the idea of an idea:

body within a body:

myth inside myth:

sword under skin:

shades of eternal night:

history lives only as long as we

write:

but vengeance—

that first fire:

look:

it still burns.

Fifty Days at Iliam: Heroes of the Ilians, 1978

X

]Still,

]it

]burns—

Untitled, III, 2008

Meditation on Communication

Dear Cy—

And why wouldn't   I go

                                        like language

                to where

                                I am

not   blue scrim   of sky and   sea

                                                                        calligraphy of memory

                                        cataract

                                                not illustration but realization

rhythm

                        wave

                                        cascade—

Have you seen   the now,   Cy?

You would not

                        could never—

The sky   sun scorched

                fire and   more fire

black as a bruise   but not   as soft

I think even   oceans

                                        are burning

                                                        or   melting

                        everything   molting

from what   it was

                        to   what it is

                going to be—

                                        tonight   my son

asked what my weird   super

                power would be   and I said

to walk into

                                a painting

                        so why   wouldn't I?

Cy?

                into

it / you go

among   the blue   trace of

the   almost   of my   name

murmur of the   visual—

you have   to me   written   so

why

how could I   not become

the blue

sky-skinned   sea-

skinned,

my body   a choir of birdsong

ready to light   up   with the

glowing wheel   of alteration   so that we

may see

far enough ahead   to go

to go

that blue   it is   beyond blue

the way   this life

is   beyond all   things coming   directly toward

so why not   among   the cataracts   lit by the   light

of not   language   but its   shadow

its   shell   as

though it too   is burned   through

to bone—

Go?

I have   driven

through flame

this is not   metaphor

and yet

it is   language   or at least

its shell

its scorch   mark   marked   look

at my   skin,

Cy,   I am   as   blue

as the iris   behind   Death's black   patch

blue   as the sky   when it changes   to   sea

Go?

I am

already there

Untitled, V, 2008

Letter of Resignation, 1959–67

Letter of Resignation

Dear Cy,

I hereby submit

my letter:

      by which I mean:
            here we are,
again before the sayable:

to say is to be, and I am tired
            of being:
of saying:
      so I submit my resignation from this:

year of agony and accrual:
year of war and warring:
year of flood and fire:
year of silence and suffering:
year of insurgence: year of instroke: year of inscription:
year of silence and more suffering:
year of yearning and more yearning:
year of losing, year of the lost, year of the least:

I hereby,
      Cy,
            regret to inform
the dead
      I am coming to join them:

please inform _____ we have from _____ resigned

resign:
late 14 c., "give up (something), surrender, abandon, submit; relinquish (an office, position, right, claim)," from Old French *resigner* "renounce, relinquish" (13 c.), from Latin *resignāre* "to check off, annul, cancel, give back, give up," from *re-,* here perhaps denoting "opposite" (see *re-*), + *signare* "to make an entry in an account book," literally "to mark," from Latin *signum* "identifying mark, sign."

Letter of Resignation, 1959–67

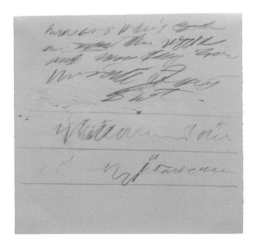

To make a mark is to sign,
                    to sign is to mark, and to mark is to make:
marking as a surrender,
                    an abandon:

I relinquish
I abandon
I submit

To mark is to renounce,
                    to surrender is to give back:
to write is to announce and renounce,
                    to say and to silence:
to address and to erase:

Dear Brothers,
I have convoked you to this Consistory.

Dear Readers,
this is my letter:
                    to the wor[l]d:

                    I am resigned to its undeliverability.

                    re: back to the original place
                    sign: gesture or motion of the hand

Dear Cy,
The beginning of writing is rupture,
a shattering into letters:

what if all writing is a form of betrayal?
what if all writing is nothing more than repetition?
what if all repetition is a form of concealment?

To write is to retrace:
what if all writing is a form of return?

Writing, says Jabès, *is never anything but a challenge to the unsayable.*

And so,

Let us say: *Kakuma*
Let us say: *Dadaab*
Let us say: *Za'atari*
Let us say: *Matamoros*
Let us write: *Kutupalong, Um Rakuba, Rukban, Moria, Idlib, Hagadera, Dagahaley, Ifo, Yida, Katumba, Pugnido,*
                Panian, Mishamo, Reynosa, Cox's Bazar, Kyiv . . .

From erasure, I hereby re-sign:
                     I hereby commit to write:

                                            write:
Old English *writan* "to score, outline, draw the figure of," later "to set down in writing" (class I strong verb; past
      tense *wrat,* past participle *writen*), from Proto-Germanic *writan* "tear, scratch" (source also of Old
           Frisian *writa* "to write," Old Saxon *writan* "to tear, scratch, write," Old Norse *rita* "write, scratch,
           outline," Old High German *rizan* "to write, scratch, tear," German *reißen* "to tear, pull, tug, sketch,
                                         draw, design").

Dear Cy,
I'm thinking of design and resign:
                      of score and scratch:
writing as tearing:
          to write is to rend:

Dear Cy,
Tell me:
          what do you want us not to see?

Homage to the aesthetics of negation—
the discourse of dissimulation.

  From what are you resigning?

And to whom do you *write*?
And what do you say through your refusal to say?
And why did you change your mind?
And what are you hiding?

Letter of Resignation, 1959–67

Scribble as both writing

                    and unwriting:

protection and occlusion:

The written page is no mirror, writes Jabès. *To write means to confront an unknown face.*

art = the revealed and the veiled:

                                                            scribble:
    mid-15 c., *scriblen,* "to write (something) quickly and carelessly, without regard to correctness or elegance," from
            Medieval Latin *scribillare,* diminutive of Latin *scribere,* "to write" (from Proto-Indo-European root
            skribh- "to cut"). Or perhaps a native formation from Middle English *scriben* "to write" (see *scribe*
            (v.)) + diminutive suffix *-el* (3). Classical Latin had *conscribillare.* The sense of "make unintelligible
                    tangled lines on paper out of idleness or for amusement" is modern.

To scribble, to strike through, to scratch out:
the opposite of erasure—
it is the mark of error,
                    the confession of confusion—
the hand drafting the draft,
                    writing that is not writing,
writing as ruse,
            deflection and disguise,
mask, shield and shelter,
meaning not through articulation but abdication—
                            no clarity, only confusion.

The writing in the trees remains illegible—

Dear Cy,
It is with great regret
                    the earth submits its resignation—
it can no longer sustain glacier sink and snow cede,
                            leaf fire, sky fire,
 water wane and water surge,
                    reef rot, sheet melt, lake lift—

*citing Katrina and Tubbs and Maria and Cedar and Caldor and Harvey and Dorian and Camp and Vamco and Laura
and Amphan and Eta and Michael and Fiona—*

Dearest Cy,

Everything is ending.

My mother, an artist, painted her final work on the cast covering my son's arm. I think about her dying every day. I feel it is impossible to write. I feel as though this book, composed almost entirely during the pandemic, is both bookended and wholly inscribed by death. Twombly is dead. My father is dead. My mother is dead. My father-in-law is dead. One of my closest friends is dead. She drank herself to death. I've not told you that before. Will you forgive me? Can you even read this? Did you notice, Cy, that in my book of poems, this section is in prose? Why do you think that is? I wonder if the equivalent for you is including text in your paintings. What if I *painted* this? Or *drew* it? Could you see it then? Dear Cy, I know I just told you my mother is dead, but I feel I need to say it again. And do you know what else? When I tried to type *dead* above, I spelled *dean*. Dear Cy, did you know that *dead* and *dean* are only one letter apart? My friend Elizabeth noticed before me that *Dean Rader* is only two letters from *Dear Reader*.

Dear Reader/Dean Rader,

~~Please accept~~ my resignation.

Letter of Resignation, 1959–67

III

What is the deepest loss that you have suffered?

Rainer Maria Rilke

Ilium (One Morning Ten Years Later), Part II, 1964

Octet

page	scrape	sketch	sky	fear	plod
end	scar	row	scorch	white	fish
dot	dash	black	wax	fight	sex
draw	spear	slash	cut	paint	filth
skin	kill	mix	slit	gash	touch
light	loss	x	bliss	bone	year
blood	sail	wind	oar	spume	wheel
spew	rip	wash	drown	one	more

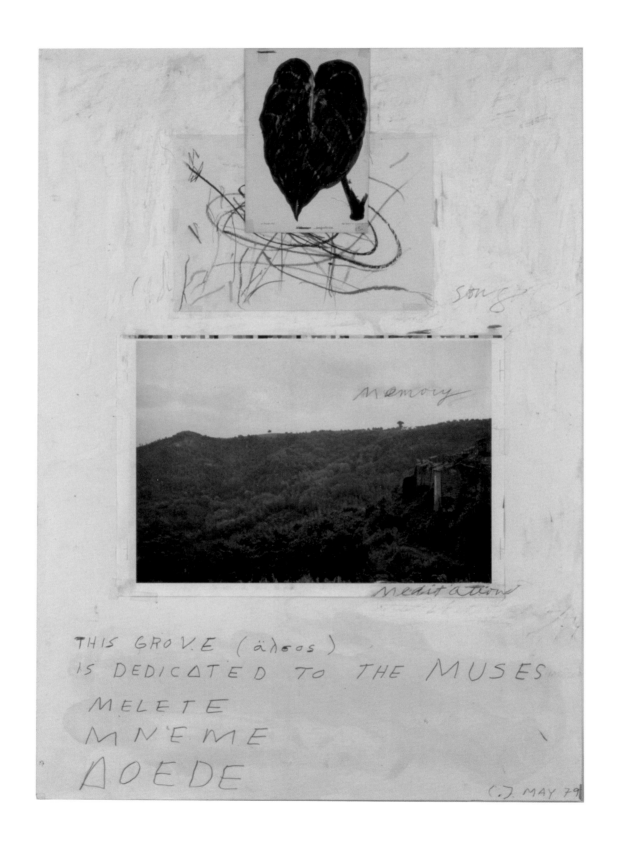

Muses, 1979

Meditation on Inspiration

This poem was going to explore the notion of painting as picture—

                    Dear Cy,

~~there is so much to say about line and color and symbol and loss.~~

                                        are you the muse?

Tiny journal of all failures?

                    ~~The more I listen the less I hear~~

———————————————————————————————————

I am thinking of Twombly in his grave

                    [one letter from *grove*]

                                        in Rome—

My father in his in Oklahoma:

                    every word a wound: a slash: a suture:

Sing in me,

          mute muse—

                    make me more than the absence where I begin.

Dear Cy,

          all writing is elegy—

Untitled, 1969

Meditation on Revolution

Morning again,
                    and the sky a litter of light lit blue,
as if a sky of sea could be black blown blue.

Nothing is clearer than at its beginning.

Before names,
                    before words roll out their knives and start to sharpen,
before the days tilt you back in their chair and ask you to open wide.

                                        I want to know what makes the hidden break
                through.

                                            I want to know what the circular
                    slides into.

                                            I want to know how we know
                    what's missing.

                                I want to know why, when I look at this painting,
            I see love.

Night Watch, 1966

Self-Portrait in the Dark

We have been out in the woods again,

                                    always, it seems,

searching for the future.

                         Twombly in a helmet with a little light on the front.

Ahead, the path is cave-colored,

                        black as a lung, and about as useless.

Whatever is on the end of my leash

                            is tugging me into the brush.

The growls stop,

                  the full moon a mic drop in the darkness.

The stage is set,

                    brighter self—

time to walk out alone.

Untitled, 1989

This Is No Time for Poetry,

so why not ask that halo
of dark whisper for anything, everything:
why not write the litany of wax and ash
on the first page of the book of
All My Shortcomings?
Haven't I lived long enough
in the bone hollow, long enough in bonebreak and brakelight?

When do I not hear the high hum of desire
along the ringing rails of the heart's train?
O Absent One,
hasn't the stillness of your voice broken my blood's black bells
hasn't its knife sliced the candlewick of my tongue?

What haven't I asked for? What haven't I stolen?

Give me sun spoor and moon melt,
give me grief's profusion,
give me heaven's crevice call—
let me gaze into what I shall not see,
let the questions,
small as seeds,
drop into the dark garden of the mind.

To silence your voice is to hear your voice:
I am listening:

Is the word *want,* is the word *breath,* is the word *no*?
Where are you, earliest annihilator?
First fist, first first, first bruise—
I feel your shunt:
mouth, who will you cry out to? Heart, who will hang your noose?

I am trying to stretch out into the nothingness that is this life,
trying to untie the rope and drift,
unmoored, into what I have lost:
to listen to the song the Angels of Infinite Distance
might be singing:
But where is the shape to hold my hearing?
I wait, will wait. I try, am trying
to listen.

Orion III, 1968

Meditation on Direction

More wave than scribble—

Why is it that Twombly always seems to be writing with his wrong hand?

a mode

of visual music: emanations, vibrations—

aural made visible:

Why is it the gods are never farther away than when we are close?

Sky-sliced and star-stamped,

descent our shape and our source.

How can so little do so much?

O to live among the livid, the dead:

everything slanted—

nothing straight, not even the path

of the path.

Untitled (Say Goodbye, Catullus, to the Shores of Asia Minor), 1994

~~Unfinished~~ Unending Journey

In the middle of our life,

                we never know it is the middle.

It terrifies my son the sea has no center and no end.

                                        [*The shining white air trembling*]

Me too.

I wonder about everything:

                      the darkness the stars stare into,

words that should have been invented, how one painting

can make God feel small, my black heart.

                                          [*the flat white sea*]

If I sailed out of this world,

                  the stars, like the body's boat, would go on without me.

And perhaps, like Rilke, arrive at the center of my own absence:

                                          [*Once for each thing*]

like the artist awash in his color's ocean:

                or the poet who won't stop praying for the silence to end:

Untitled (To Sappho), 1976

Meditation on Remembering

As if life itself were wrung like
rain from the evening air—drenched in a
mist of what's missing: a hyacinth
in gray scale or windy gaps in
the erased spaces where the
dotted line of lineated mountains
once stood. I imagine your poems—trampled
and hoof-hewn, rent and riven by
a great beast not even the godlike shepherds
could contain. How. Then. Now. Once. Until.
Nothing is ever wholly whole. We are only
that which survives, even in our absence, like a
night sky the sinking sun streaks with purple.
How to say in a poem that Breonna Taylor's death is a stain
on a country, yes, but also on history? Tell me: what remains?
What endures beyond the blurred words of men on
duty? In office? You once wrote: *Those I treat well are the*
ones who most of all harm me. O lost ones: I ask to end with any word but *ground.*

Untitled, 1971

Unfinished Sonnet

I've been thinking about lines of music as furrows in a field.

I've been thinking about paper as a field of pure becoming without being.

I've been thinking about transition—

                              show me where absence stops.

I used to know what the pencil wanted.

I felt I knew what the hand needed from the brush.

I felt I thought the way birds know air—

                              everything is transference:

Untitled, 1963–64

Eternal Return

To circle, to conceal, to center:
to master the descent into disorder—

      (*spiral swirl arc of the heavens*)

to dissolve into a map
of your own making—

      (*cartography of camouflage blur and blotch X marks the _____*)

an internal orbit of excess—
orphic and oceanic all at once,

      (*citation of destruction annotation of eradication*)

both vortex and veil:
chaos + pattern = the possible

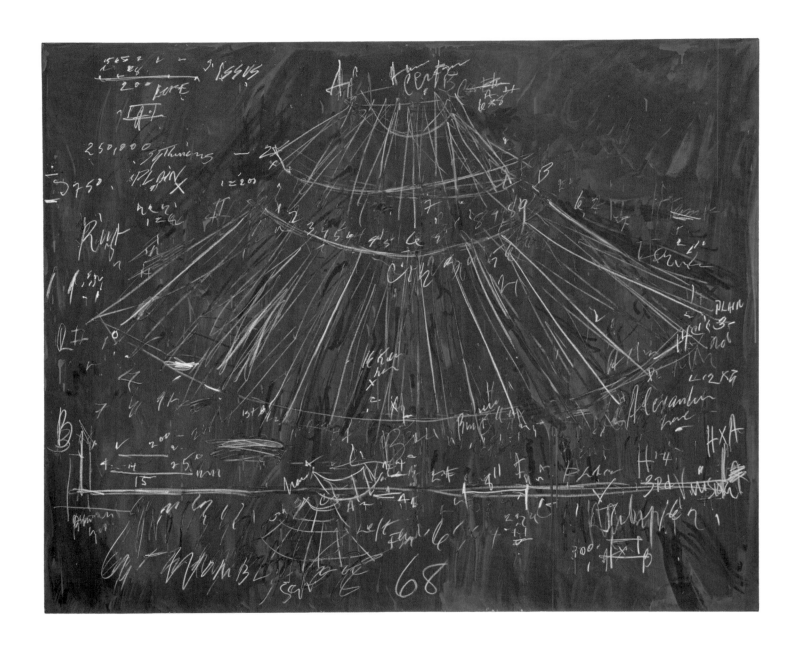

Synopsis of a Battle, 1968

Meditation on Creation

Synopsis of a Battle

as a diagram of God's becoming—

a chart of the battle to *be,* an advancement from absence

[into presence]—as though existence is an incursion, a plan of attack on the

uncreated by an army of singular lineation, drawn downward, obscure as an

outline, yet radiant [effulgent even] in its precision, its calculation of complete invasion—

both flex and flux, fall and flow—eternal alluvium flooding the world entire—a divine darkness

lit by its own duration—illuminated not only by scheme but also by signs, secret

script of the afterlife, hidden and holy, revealing nothing to the unworthy [which I am]—

[*nothing I make will be this great*]—and so to the absence [to it] [to him?] I bow

Orpheus, 1975

In Advance of All Parting

Another canvas,

        another blank page—

more of the same: absence within absence,

          uncertainty and indeterminacy,

    those twins language lifts out of.

        What came first—drawing or writing?

Every sign is a symbol of its vanishing,

          every mark the beginning of its erasure.

    Among the waning,

        I want to be the singing glass that shivers as it rings,

    both the tracing and the trace—

          I want to be the mark that marks our names.

Untitled, 1971

Meditation on Inscription

Within the writing there are no words—

no language, no signs,

            not even the notion of signs—

only the notion of notation:

               and yet still there is instruction:

black lines on a white page,

             white lines on a black board.

All chaos is a form of learning,

              all learning a form of chaos—

Twombly knew that form is itself a form of language

                    and language an instruction of words—

a lesson on what may and may not be *meant*

                by writing.

Consider that writing is more than what it does not say,

just as drawing is more than what it does not illustrate.

               This, viewer,

is what I am thinking as I imagine you in front of this painting—

             lost in the swirl of signifier and signified,

the mind patterning the possible.

            Perhaps you see a black field of white wheat,

or snow strings across the windshield,

                              the strange stenography of the stars,

a sacred text,

                 both code and codex,

slate of rejected numbers,

                    forgotten letters,

formulas for flight and infinitude,

                         lost alphabet of the first speakers,

asemic symbols of their absence,

                    of ours.

Exhumed and erased,

                    exhumed and erased:

found again—

              begun—

                    by nothing but your own looking.

Consider:

        language begins at the moment language becomes a question.

Consider:

        words begin with their own nothingness.

Consider:

        art, like life, begins in the void.

Reader,

you and I stand once more before the borderless—

let us dissolve into it together.

Orpheus, 1979

Once Again in Thought about Rilke, Twombly's Orpheus Paintings, and Fatherhood,
I Consider the Inevitability of Creation and Loss

Scarred sky,

   the last beams bruised beneath the surface of stars.

  The whole world a contusion

     slowly transforming from one thing

  to the next—

    the one cell, the one life,

always becoming two:

    What if it is the sun that follows the moon?

How do we know we're not the bridle

     hard against the teeth of this life?

Just because something has a saddle
     doesn't mean we should ride it.

What would it take to be inside the music

      the cello does not know how to play?

  What would it take to say to the strings

       make me silent?

What would it take for the skin to sing

     its own song of blood and blooming?

To know one truth is to know nothing.

To wear your nothingness,

   well, now we're getting somewhere.

I once believed I could be lifted by language out of language.

I once believed the horse hooves in the distance

                                        were the ocean telling the rocks about water.

I once believed loss would thread my mind's needle like a blind seamstress.

But that was a long time ago.

Now,

        I understand that time is nothing more than pure duration,

& that the mind is a field of herons

                        who have lost their way.

Even so,

        I will let the entire lie down in my body's blue light

in hope that something will start

                        to heal.

Gary Rader, In Memoriam (1946–2017)

IV

Those who depend upon the intellect are the many.

Those who depend upon perception alone are the few.

Agnes Martin

Ut pictura poesis
Horace

My father, Gary Rader, died in December 2017, three days before Christmas. He had been a successful public figure—a popular mayor of my hometown, president of the local Kiwanis club, a state-champion baseball coach, an auctioneer, a bail bondsman, a 32nd degree Mason. Once, he even won a hog-calling competition. He was survived by far more than us. He lived on in numerous newspaper clippings, dozens of plaques and tokens of appreciation for volunteerism, framed photos of him with athletes, musicians, and other politicians. Volunteer of the Year. Mayor of the Year. Mentor of the Year. In addition to his public persona, which I knew, he also survived through the micro details of his private life, which I felt: souvenirs from travels, stuffed animals, watches, pens, ties, cuff links. My sister and I spent several days going through his effects, and I kept asking the same question: *What makes a life?*

Not long after, in early 2018, I made a cross-country trip to New York to see the first retrospective of drawings and works on paper by the American artist Cy Twombly. Gorgeously presented at the Gagosian galleries, the exhibit, a life's work, bore the title *In Beauty It Is Finished: Drawings 1951–2008.* The title refers to a Navajo prayer, but to me, it signified the end of my father's life.

It is finished.

A life's work.

I have been taken with Twombly for over thirty years, but I don't think I was prepared for the deep emotions his work would ignite. As I moved through this career-spanning exhibit, I kept finding parallels between the act of looking at the effects of Twombly's life and the act of looking through the effects of my father's.

In the case of Twombly, I wanted to see what a life devoted to art looked and felt like. Twombly's work has always been deeply elegiac, and in those drawings, I found what I have come to think of as masterful mourning. Entering his visual fields of pictures and poetry helped me process my father's death as nothing else had. I saw a big mind and big talent trying to come to terms with meaning, life, death, the weight of history, and the ability of art to put us in touch with that which is beyond articulation. In those pieces, almost all of which blurred the line between text and image, I recognized Twombly's refusal to choose between the two modes of expression. As though poetry somehow both enhances and expands art's grasp. As though the images and text both desired, to quote Rilke, "to rise again into pure relation."

That was not the first time I made a Twombly pilgrimage. In 1995, the Cy Twombly Gallery opened at the Menil Collection in Houston, and I took a detour from a cross-country road trip to visit it and the much more famous Rothko Chapel. To my great surprise, I found the Twombly Gallery and Twombly's work more spiritually alive. The Twomblys were active and chaotic and turbulent. They were soaring and searching. Many contained words from poems but were nevertheless unreadable, inscrutable. And in their inscrutability, their inaccessibility, I felt the presence of the divine, itself inscrutable and inaccessible. I saw Twombly groping for meaning, relevance, connection, expression by way of two different but interrelated acts—drawing and writing. Images were not enough. Poetry was not enough. I believed I had been shown some sort of map that would, one day, reveal something to me: a way, a path, a direction.

That sensation returned twenty-five years later at the Gagosian, heavy with the weight of my father's passing, but perhaps even more revelatory. It was as if someone gave me a meal, but I did not know I had been starving. Or that I had suddenly learned to see, not knowing I had lost my sight. It was as if I had known these works all along but was seeing them for the first time. After leaving the show, I went for a walk on the High Line in the Chelsea dusk before heading back to my hotel room where, in the near darkness, I began penning a series of questions to my father and to Twombly. The next morning, I opened my notebook to see what I had written, and before I knew it, I was working on a poem that talked to one of the pieces in the exhibit. That became the opening poem in this collection, and now: the book you hold.

Why Twombly? This is an impossible question to answer, though I have tried in these pages to place Twombly's work in a personal context. Put even more directly: I absolutely and completely adore his work. I feel about it the way I feel about Rilke's *Duino Elegies* or how others feel about the Sistine Chapel or Machu Picchu or Beethoven's Ninth Symphony or the 23rd Psalm. In Twombly's work I see the faded traces, the disappearing spiraling spoor of something sacred. One day, during the pandemic, my wife came downstairs well before sunup to find me deeply immersed in several pages of Twombly's *Letter of Resignation. What are you doing?* she asked. *Looking for answers,* I responded.

It is that poetics of seeking that draws me to Twombly. I think of Twombly's artworks as struggling poems trying to cover all kinds of emotions—anger, fear, excitement, aggression, regret, beauty, intensity, and ambition. Indeed, his work mimics both a poem and the act of reading a poem. Traditionally a page is just a setting for the black type of text, but here, the negative space of the page and the positive space of print strive to create a scene as dynamic, as interdependent, as a Twombly canvas. Or, put another way: What if Twombly's images are the poems and my writing the illustrations?

"The terrible thing about art," writes Rilke, "is that the further you go into it the more you are pledged to attempt the uttermost, the almost impossible." To me, the success of Twombly's work—its gestural and emotional brilliance—is itself almost impossible. How can so little do so much? How can the same drawing resemble both urban graffiti and a sacred illuminated text? How can one thing both ask to be read and refuse to be read? Twombly's paintings and drawings are meditations on what is possible to communicate through the marriage of the visual and lexical. Ultimately, his greatness lies in his paradoxical ability to simultaneously fill and empty a canvas, the way art both fills and empties a life. My ambition is that these poems name and celebrate that impossibility.

———————

The final public outing I made before the coronavirus lockdown of 2020 was a return visit to the Twombly Gallery at the Menil. When I met the curator, Michelle White, in early March, I knew without knowing that something was coming. I spent two hours in the gallery, moving from room to room, taking notes, asking questions. I stood for who knows how long in front of *Say Goodbye, Catullus,* scribbling down lines from Rilke's *Duino Elegies* that Twombly had himself scribbled into the painting decades before. In that room on that day this book began to take shape, not just as an idea but as a necessity.

On the last flight out of Houston that night, Twombly, Rilke, my father, and the future of the earth were fighting for my focus. I felt like death was everywhere. I had no idea what was—in so many ways—to come. I pulled out my copy of the *Duino Elegies* and turned directly to the Ninth Elegy, arguably the most joyful elegy in the history of writing. I thought of Rilke, Twombly, my father—that furious trinity of ghosts haunting. Helping. Healing.

What makes a life?

I felt inexpressible grief and realized the futility and utter necessity of art, as though the plane were falling while flying or flying while falling. But then I looked back at the Rilke, and as if by some miracle, landed on one of my favorite lines in all of poetry: Here *is the time for the* sayable, here *is its homeland.*

The final sentence on the previous page is where this epilogue originally ended.

That was in November 2021.

A few weeks later, roughly a month after I completed the first draft of this book, my mother contracted COVID-19. She likely brought it with her from Oklahoma, or caught it somewhere on her journey to visit our family in San Francisco, or, more tragically, from one of us.

We will never know for sure.

Just a couple of days after she returned home, she and my mother-in-law tested positive. The next day, my wife tested positive, then my oldest son, then me, and then, on December 31, our youngest son. A few hours later, my mother was admitted to Mercy Hospital in Oklahoma City. She never left. These events transpired on the final day of 2021, ensuring we would never forget the unflinching brutality of one of the worst years in recent memory.

Early in the morning of January 5, 2022, less than two weeks after leaving our house and less than two hours after I left her hospital room, my mother died of complications from COVID-19. I was able to spend her final day by her bedside reading her favorite passages from the Bible and my favorite passages from Rilke's *Duino Elegies.*

Though I walk through the valley of the shadow of death, I read.
For thou art with me, I read.
Surely, I read, *goodness and mercy shall follow me all the days of my life,* I said.

Praise this world to the angel, I read.
And I read: *Show him how happy a Thing can be, how innocent and ours,*
how even lamenting grief purely decides to take form,
serves as a Thing, or dies into a Thing—, and blissfully
escapes far beyond the violin.

Late that night, in the heavy dark of the Oklahoma City hospital room, my mother's chest heaving as though her entire body was a lung of lead, I held her hand and read her the final poem in this book, hoping the last lines, offered as a kind of prayer, might save my mother's life. They did not.

And now this *Thing,* to invoke Rilke again, which began with the death of my father and concluded with the death of my mother, is in your hands. This book is for you, reader, but in it—and now in you—is them.

Notes

"In Which Twombly and Rader Consider the Letter" appeared in *Dear America: Letters of Hope, Habitat, Defiance, and Democracy.* The column on the right comes from the *Oxford English Dictionary* entry for "letter."

"Meditation on Circulation" borrows two lines from a poem by Wallace Stevens—"The Pleasures of Merely Circulating"—that seems to perfectly describe much of Twombly's scrawl work.

"~~Sonnet~~: The Inscrutability of Influence" talks to and samples "Ode to Psyche" by John Keats, as does Twombly's drawing.

"Elegies (Variations)" is in memory of my mother, Ginger Rader, who died in January 2022. It responds to Twombly's *Variations on the Elegies.* I believe Twombly's drawing is a homage to Rilke's *Duino Elegies.* There are ten Duino elegies, and there are ten boxes in the drawing. Rilke was translating Paul Valéry when he died. My belief is that Twombly's work is an elegy to both poets—an elegy to elegists. In my poem, I wanted each stanza to correspond both to one of the ten Twombly boxes and to one of the ten *Duino Elegies.* I set myself the following tasks: each boxlike stanza is composed of four lines of four words, and each also contains a phrase from the corresponding Duino elegy: a double tribute. The poem also imports a line from Robert Hass's "Meditation at Lagunitas."

"The Fire That Consumes All before It" is a kind of modified crown in ten parts that corresponds to the ten panels of Twombly's epic *Fifty Days at Iliam* in the Philadelphia Museum of Art. Twombly's work is a response to Alexander Pope's translation of *Iliad*—in particular, the final fifty days of the Battle of Troy. The *Iliad* contains what is considered Western literature's first example of ekphrasis, a term from Greek that means "writing about art." There is a fascinating moment in book 18, where Homer stops talking about war and begins to describe in glorious detail the shield of Achilles—which gives its name to the first panel in Twombly's cycle. It is as though Twombly is pointing to the foundational symbol of ekphrasis but executing its reversal: instead of writing poetry about art, he is making art about poetry. Section 7 quotes Pope's translation as well as Samuel Johnson on that translation. According to World Population Review, thirty-two nations are presently at war.

"Meditation on Direction" steals a line from Cole Swensen's terrific essay on Twombly, "Cy Twombly, *Hero & Leander* 1981–84."

"~~Unfinished~~ Unending Journey" enters into conversation with Twombly's massive *Untitled (Say Goodbye, Catullus, to the Shores of Asia Minor)* at the Menil's Cy Twombly Gallery. In the painting, Twombly scrawls lines from poets including Catullus and Rilke, specifically from the Ninth Elegy from *Duino Elegies.* My poem incorporates and adapts lines that Twombly has imported into his work.

"Meditation on Remembering" is a golden shovel, a relatively new form created by Terrance Hayes in which the last word in each line of a poem creates (or recreates) a previously published poem. In this case, if you read just the last word in each line of my poem, from top to bottom, it replicates the Sappho fragment in the Twombly drawing.

4: *Orpheus,* 1979 (courtesy of Emanuel Hoffmann Foundation, on permanent loan to the Öffentliche Kunstsammlung Basel; photo: Kunstsammlung Basel, Martin P. Bühler)

6: *Untitled,* 1970 (courtesy of Archives Fondazione Nicola Del Roscio; photo: Mimmo Capone)

8: *Untitled,* detail, 1970

10: *Nini's Painting,* 1971 (courtesy of The Broad)

12: *Note I* from *Three Notes from Salalah,* 2005–07 (courtesy of The Doris and Donald Fisher Collection at the San Francisco Museum of Modern Art)

14: *Beyond (A System for Passing), Part X,* 1971 (courtesy of Cy Twombly Foundation)

16: *Untitled,* 1970 (courtesy of Museum of Modern Art, acquired through the Lillie P. Bliss Bequest and The Sidney and Harriet Janis Collection, both by exchange)

18: *Untitled,* 1967 (courtesy of the Menil Collection, Houston; gift of the artist; photo: Paul Hester)

20: *Ode to Psyche,* 1960 (courtesy of Cy Twombly Foundation; photo: Giorgio Benni, Rome)

22: *Untitled,* 1969 (courtesy of Cy Twombly Foundation)

24: *Mars and the Artist,* 1975 (courtesy of Cy Twombly Foundation)

26: *Cold Stream,* 1966 (courtesy of Galerie Karsten Greve; photo: Jochen Littkemann)

28: *Untitled,* 1966 (courtesy of Cy Twombly Foundation)

30: *Untitled (Variations on the Elegies),* 1966 (courtesy of Cy Twombly Foundation)

34: *Poems to the Sea,* 1959 (courtesy of Cy Twombly Foundation)

38–56: The *Fifty Days at Iliam* paintings appear courtesy of Philadelphia Museum of Art, gift (by exchange) of Samuel S. White 3rd and Vera White, 1989. Titles are listed below.

> *Fifty Days at Iliam: Shield of Achilles,* 1978
> *Fifty Days at Iliam: Heroes of the Achaeans,* 1978
> *Fifty Days at Iliam: Vengeance of Achilles,* 1978
> *Fifty Days at Iliam: Achaeans in Battle,* 1978
> *Fifty Days at Iliam: The Fire That Consumes All before It,* 1978
> *Fifty Days at Iliam: Shades of Achilles, Patroclus, and Hector,* 1978
> *Fifty Days at Iliam: House of Priam,* 1978
> *Fifty Days at Iliam: Ilians in Battle,* 1978
> *Fifty Days at Iliam: Shades of Eternal Night,* 1978
> *Fifty Days at Iliam: Heroes of the Ilians,* 1978

58: *Untitled, III,* 2008 (courtesy of the Department of Culture and Tourism, Abu Dhabi; photo: APF)

61: *Untitled, V,* 2008 (courtesy of the Department of Culture and Tourism, Abu Dhabi; photo: APF)

62, 64, 65, 68, 70, and 71: *Letter of Resignation,* 1959–67 (courtesy of Cy Twombly Foundation)

74: *Ilium (One Morning Ten Years Later), Part II,* 1964 (courtesy of Gagosian)

76: *Muses,* 1979 (courtesy of Cy Twombly Foundation)

78: *Untitled,* 1969 (courtesy of Cy Twombly Foundation)

80: *Night Watch,* 1966 (courtesy of Galerie Karsten Greve; photo: Jochen Littkemann)

82: *Untitled,* 1989 (courtesy of Cy Twombly Foundation)

84: *Orion III,* 1968 (courtesy of Udo and Anette Brandhorst Collection, Bayerische Staatsgemäldesammlungen, Museum Brandhorst, Munich; photo: Haydar Koyupinar)

86: *Untitled (Say Goodbye, Catullus, to the Shores of Asia Minor),* 1994 (courtesy of the Menil Collection, Houston; gift of the artist; photo: Paul Hester)

88: *Untitled (To Sappho),* 1976 (courtesy of Gagosian)

90: *Untitled,* 1971 (courtesy of Cy Twombly Foundation; photo: Belisario Manicone, Rome)

92: *Untitled,* 1963–64 (courtesy of Galerie Karsten Greve)

94: *Synopsis of a Battle,* 1968 (courtesy of Virginia Museum of Fine Arts; gift of Sydney and Frances Lewis)

96: *Orpheus,* 1975 (courtesy of Cy Twombly Foundation)

98: *Untitled,* 1971 (courtesy of the Doris and Donald Fisher Collection at the San Francisco Museum of Modern Art and the San Francisco Museum of Modern Art, fractional purchase through gift)

102: *Orpheus,* 1979 (courtesy of Cy Twombly Foundation)

Acknowledgments

Thank you to the following publications—and their editors—where versions of these poems first appeared, some in radically different form and with different titles:

Air/Light: "Eternal Return," "Meditation on Communication," "Meditation on Revision," and "Self-Portrait in the Dark"

Bennington Review: "Meditation on Absolution" and "Meditation on Remembering"

Brick: "Studies for Excursus"

The Cincinnati Review: "This Is No Time for Poetry,"

Harvard Review: "In Advance of All Parting" and "~~Sonnet:~~ The Inscrutability of Influence"

Kestrel: "Meditation on Inspiration"

Narrative: "Meditation on Inscription"

New England Review: "Once Again in Thought about Rilke, Twombly's Orpheus Paintings, and Fatherhood, I Consider the Inevitability of Creation and Loss" and "Troubled by Thoughts about Infinity and Oblivion, I Exit the Twombly Retrospective at Dusk and Walk the High Line with the Ghost of My Father"

On the Seawall: "Meditation on Comprehension," "Meditation on Direction," "Meditation on Motion," and "Octet"

The Southern Review: "Meditation on Mimesis"

Waxwing: "Unending Octet"

West Marin Review: "Meditation on Revolution"

The West Review: "Meditation on Circulation"

ZYZZYVA: "System" and "Unfinished Sonnet"

"In Which Twombly and Rader Consider the Letter" appeared in *Dear America: Letters of Hope, Habitat, Defiance, and Democracy,* edited by Simmons Buntin, Elizabeth Dodd, and Derek Sheffield (Trinity University Press, 2020).

Very special thank you to Nicola Del Roscio and Eleonora Di Erasmo from the Cy Twombly Foundation for their astonishing support for this entire project from the very beginning. Their graciousness regarding permission and the reproduction of the Twombly images literally made this book happen. It would not exist without them. It is impossible for me to adequately convey my gratitude.

Thank you to Michael Wiegers, Elizabeth Ash, Claretta Holsey, John Pierce, Elaina Ellis, Ryo Yamaguchi, and everyone at Copper Canyon. Thanks to Jessica Roeder and Rowan Sharp for a heavy copyediting lift. Huge thanks to Phil Kovacevich for his brilliant design work. I am eternally indebted to the entire Copper Canyon family for your belief in and support of this book.

Thank you to the following organizations that made writing and funding this work possible: the Solomon R. Guggenheim Foundation, the MacDowell Foundation, Headlands Center for the Arts, Art Omi, and the University of San Francisco. Thank you to Deans Marcelo Camperi, Eileen Chia-Ching Fung, and Jeffrey Paris for their support with writing retreats and faculty release time. Thank you to all my colleagues at the University of San Francisco.

Thank you to Jordan Kantor for his invaluable, incessant, and unending counsel during my Twombly obsessions. I'm not sure this book would exist without him. Thank you to Victoria Chang for reading and commenting on this book in manuscript. Thank you to Ashley Cardona, Brian Clements, Brian Komei Dempster, Judy Halebsky, Chris Haven, Amorak Huey, W. Todd Kaneko, Amy Norkus, Christina Olson, and Jean Prokott, who saw many of these poems in early iterations. Thank you to Brandon Brown, Laura Cogan, Carol Edgarian, Forrest Gander, Elizabeth Savage, Jonathan Silverman, and Oscar Villalon. Gratitude and admiration for Thomas Ingmire, who transformed some of these poems into a gorgeous book of Twomblyesque calligraphy.

Big thanks to all of the permissions people at the many museums who provided images and information about the works, in particular David Rozelle (SFMoMA), Donna McClendon (Menil), Tamara Cabur (Louvre Abu Dhabi), Howell Perkins (Virginia Museum of Fine Arts), Adele Minardi (Gagosian), and Raffaele Valente (Cy Twombly Foundation).

Lastly, thank you to my wife, Jill Ramsey, and my sons, Gavin and Henry, who not only supported the purchase of endless catalogues raisonnés but also had to endure oh so many trips to galleries and museums, so that their husband and father could gaze at what Henry once dubbed "scribble scrabble."

My mother and father would have loved this book. It is dedicated to their memories.

About the Author

Dean Rader's most recent book from Copper Canyon Press, *Self-Portrait as Wikipedia Entry* (2017), was a finalist for the Oklahoma Book Award and the Northern California Book Award. His debut collection of poems, *Works & Days,* won the 2010 T.S. Eliot Poetry Prize, was a finalist for the Bush Memorial Prize, and won the Texas Institute of Letters Poetry Prize. His 2014 collection *Landscape Portrait Figure Form* was named by the *Barnes & Noble Review* as a Best Poetry Book. Often engaging in collaborative projects, Rader is the coauthor of a book of sonnets, *Suture,* written with Simone Muench; the coeditor, with Brian Clements and Alexandra Teague, of *Bullets into Bells: Poets and Citizens Respond to Gun Violence*; the coeditor, with CMarie Fuhrman, of *Native Voices: Indigenous American Poetry, Craft, and Conversation*; and a co-contributor, with Victoria Chang, to *Two Roads: Poetry Reviews in Dialogue,* an innovative book review column for the *Los Angeles Review of Books.* In 2020, Rader was a finalist for the Balakian Award from the National Book Critics Circle. In 2021, he began the popular web video series Poems That Changed Me. His writing has been supported by fellowships from Princeton University, Harvard University, the MacDowell Foundation, Art Omi, the Headlands Center for the Arts, and the John R. Solomon Guggenheim Foundation, where he was a 2019 Fellow in Poetry. Rader is a professor at the University of San Francisco and lives in San Francisco with his wife and two sons.

Also by Dean Rader

Native Voices: Indigenous American Poetry, Craft and Conversations (with CMarie Fuhrman)

They Said: A Multi-Genre Anthology of Contemporary Collaborative Writing (with Simone Muench and assistant editors Sally Ashton and Jackie White)

The World Is a Text: Visual and Popular Culture (with Jonathan Silverman)

Suture (collaborative poems with Simone Muench)

Self-Portrait as Wikipedia Entry

99 Poems for the 99 Percent: An Anthology of Poetry

Landscape Portrait Figure Form

Engaged Resistance: American Indian Art, Literature, and Film from Alcatraz to the NMAI

Works & Days

Speak to Me Words: Essays on Contemporary American Indian Poetry (with Janice Gould)

Poetry is vital to language and living. Since 1972, Copper Canyon Press has published extraordinary poetry from around the world to engage the imaginations and intellects of readers, writers, booksellers, librarians, teachers, students, and donors.

WE ARE GRATEFUL FOR THE MAJOR SUPPORT PROVIDED BY:

Richard Andrews and Colleen Chartier
Anonymous
Jill Baker and Jeffrey Bishop
Anne and Geoffrey Barker
Donna Bellew
Matthew Bellew
Sarah Bird
Will Blythe
John Branch
Diana Broze
Sarah Cavanaugh
Keith Cowan and Linda Walsh
Stephanie Ellis-Smith and
    Douglas Smith
Mimi Gardner Gates
Gull Industries Inc. on behalf of
    William True
The Trust of Warren A. Gummow
William R. Hearst III
Carolyn and Robert Hedin
David and Jane Hibbard
Bruce S. Kahn
Phil Kovacevich and Eric Wechsler
Lakeside Industries Inc. on behalf of
    Jeanne Marie Lee

Maureen Lee and Mark Busto
Peter Lewis and Johanna Turiano
Ellie Mathews and Carl Youngmann as
    The North Press
Larry Mawby and Lois Bahle
Hank and Liesel Meijer
Jack Nicholson
Petunia Charitable Fund and
    adviser Elizabeth Hebert
Madelyn Pitts
Suzanne Rapp and Mark Hamilton
Adam and Lynn Rauch
Emily and Dan Raymond
Joseph C. Roberts
Jill and Bill Ruckelshaus
Cynthia Sears
Kim and Jeff Seely
Nora Hutton Shepard
D.D. Wigley
Joan F. Woods
Barbara and Charles Wright
In honor of C.D. Wright,
    from Forrest Gander
Caleb Young as C. Young Creative
The dedicated interns and faithful
    volunteers of Copper Canyon Press

TO LEARN MORE ABOUT UNDERWRITING COPPER CANYON PRESS TITLES,
PLEASE CALL 360-385-4925 EXT. 103

The pressmark for Copper Canyon Press
suggests entrance, connection, and interaction
while holding at its center
an attentive, dynamic space for poetry.

This book is set in Akzidenz Grotesk and Adobe Garamond Pro.
Book design by Phil Kovacevich.
Printed in Canada on archival-quality paper.